BETTER TOGETHER: ANIMAL GROUPS

FISH SCHOOLS

by Karen Latchana Kenney

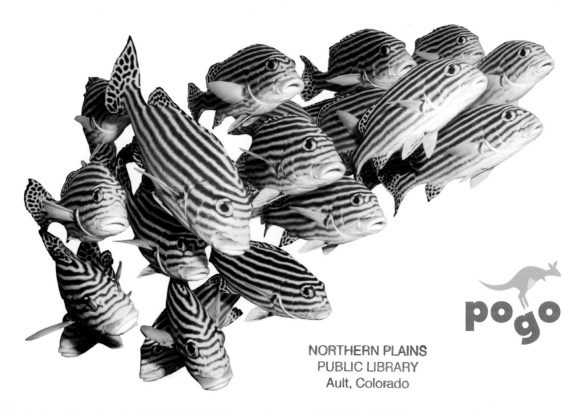

pogo

Ideas for Parents and Teachers

Pogo Books let children practice reading informational text while introducing them to nonfiction features such as headings, labels, sidebars, maps, and diagrams, as well as a table of contents, glossary, and index.

Carefully leveled text with a strong photo match offers early fluent readers the support they need to succeed.

Before Reading

- "Walk" through the book and point out the various nonfiction features. Ask the student what purpose each feature serves.
- Look at the glossary together. Read and discuss the words.

Read the Book

- Have the child read the book independently.
- Invite him or her to list questions that arise from reading.

After Reading

- Discuss the child's questions. Talk about how he or she might find answers to those questions.
- Prompt the child to think more. Ask: What did you know about fish schools before reading this book? What more would you like to learn about them?

Pogo Books are published by Jump!
5357 Penn Avenue South
Minneapolis, MN 55419
www.jumplibrary.com

Library of Congress Cataloging-in-Publication Data

Names: Kenney, Karen Latchana, author.
Title: Fish schools / by Karen Latchana Kenney.
Description: Pogo books edition.
Minneapolis, MN: Jump!, Inc., [2020]
Series: Better together: animal groups
Audience: Age 7–10. | Includes index.
Identifiers: LCCN 2018055363 (print)
LCCN 2018056503 (ebook)
ISBN 9781641288460 (ebook)
ISBN 9781641288453 (hardcover : alk. paper)
Subjects: LCSH: Fishes–Schooling–Juvenile literature.
Classification: LCC QL639.3 (ebook)
LCC QL639.3 .K46 2020 (print) | DDC 597.15–dc23
LC record available at https://lccn.loc.gov/2018055363

Editor: Jenna Trnka
Designer: Jenna Casura

Photo Credits: Rich Carey/Shutterstock, cover; Hendrik Martens/Shutterstock, 1; inusuke/iStock, 3; Leonardo Gonzalez/Shutterstock, 4; Andrea Izzotti/Shutterstock, 5; aquapix/Shutterstock, 6-7; RuthBlack/iStock, 8-9; digitalbalance/Shutterstock, 10; Alina Maieru/Shutterstock, 11; John_Walker/Shutterstock, 12-13; Steve Bloom Images/Alamy, 14-15; Erik Lornie/Alamy, 16; imageBROKER/Alamy, 17; Minden Pictures/SuperStock, 18-19; tunart/iStock, 20-21; atese/iStock, 23.

Printed in the United States of America at Corporate Graphics in North Mankato, Minnesota.

TABLE OF CONTENTS

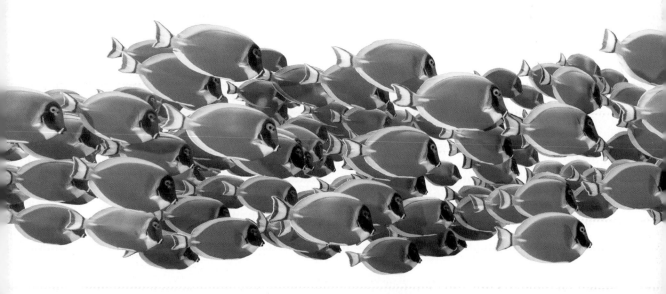

CHAPTER 1

SURVIVAL SKILLS

A silver cloud twists and turns in the ocean. It changes shape as it moves. This is not one creature. What is it?

sardines

It is a **school** of millions of sardines. The fish stay close. They move together in the same direction. Being in a group helps them survive.

Most of the world's fish live in schools. Why? Fish have few places to hide in the big ocean. **Predators** lurk nearby. These include sharks, dolphins, and larger fish. The many eyes of the school all watch for predators.

DID YOU KNOW?

Herring schools are the largest fish schools. One school can have more than 100 million herring!

Hunting one fish is easy. It is alone and gone in one bite. But hunting a group of fish is harder. Why?

One fish senses a predator. It moves. The others in the school quickly follow its movement to escape. It is harder for a predator to grab one.

TAKE A LOOK!

How do fish sense predators? They have special hairs.
They are on a line across the fish's body. These hairs
feel movement.

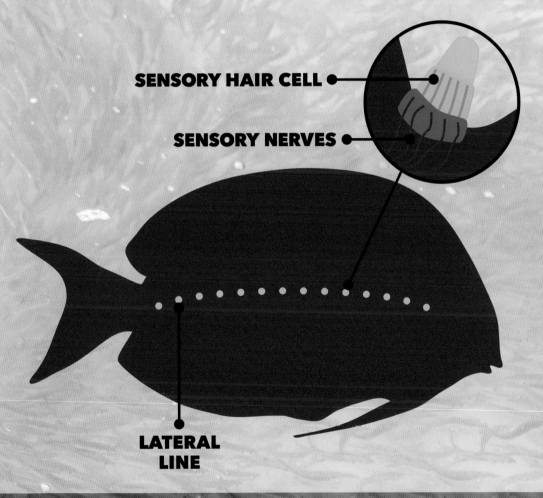

SENSORY HAIR CELL

SENSORY NERVES

**LATERAL
LINE**

CHAPTER 2

MANY MOUTHS

Finding food as a group is also easier. The school searches for tiny creatures. These **plankton** float in the water. They try to avoid the fish.

plankton ·····▶

But a school has many mouths. The fish swim with their mouths open. The plankton may move away from one fish but then end up in another fish's mouth.

shoal

Some fish stop to eat. They form a looser group. This kind of group is a **shoal**. The fish don't move in the same direction. There is more space between them.

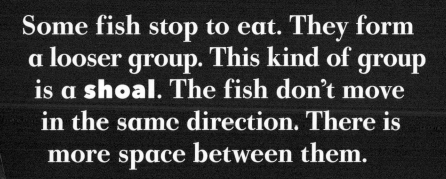

DID YOU KNOW?

Schools are made of one kind of fish. Shoals may have a few kinds of fish.

What if food is hard to find? Being in a group helps. Groups of fish find food faster. Many eyes look. Many bodies sense moving water. The fish are smarter in a group. They copy their neighbors. They move to the food together.

CHAPTER 3

MOVING FISH

Living in a school makes producing **offspring** easier, too. How? Males and females are closer together. The females lay eggs. The males **fertilize** the eggs.

eggs

Baby fish **hatch** out of the eggs.
They will form their own schools.

salmon

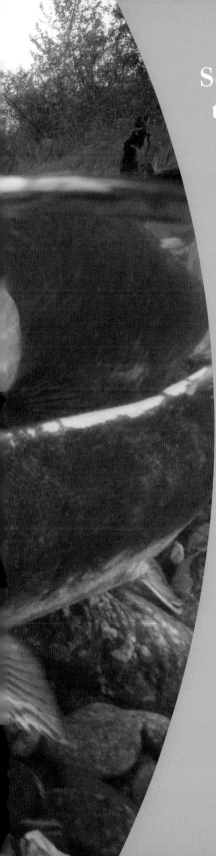

Some fish schools travel thousands of miles together. They **migrate** to find food. They also do it to **spawn** in special places. Some fish, like salmon, migrate from oceans to rivers.

DID YOU KNOW?

Adult salmon schools swim from the ocean to rivers or streams. They return to where they were born. Why? This is where they lay their eggs.

Scientists think fish in schools use less **energy**. Fish in the front cut through the water. They pave the way for the fish behind them. The fish behind don't have to use as much energy to swim through the water. This can help the group swim faster, too.

Swimming in schools helps fish in many ways. They live longer with each other.

ACTIVITIES & TOOLS

FISH MOTION

Fish schools move fast. Try this activity to see what it's like to move in a group.

What You Need:
- a few friends
- a big empty space

❶ Gather a few friends together. Have one friend stand apart from the group.

❷ When the friend that is separate shouts "go," the school has to turn. They have to try to all move together. But they have to guess which way to go by watching one another.

❸ Get the group moving. Try to move as fast as you can.

❹ Is it hard to move in the same direction? Try making a signal. Try different ways to solve the problem. Can you find a good way to know where to go? How does your school communicate?

GLOSSARY

energy: The ability or strength to do things without getting tired.

fertilize: To begin reproduction by joining sperm and egg cells.

hatch: To break out of an egg.

migrate: To move to another area or climate at a particular time of year.

offspring: The young of an animal.

plankton: Tiny animals and plants that drift or float in oceans and lakes.

predators: Animals that hunt other animals for food.

school: A tight group of fish that swims and feeds together.

shoal: A loose group of fish whose members swim and feed near one another.

spawn: To produce or release eggs.

INDEX

TO LEARN MORE

Finding more information is as easy as 1, 2, 3.

❶ Go to www.factsurfer.com

❷ Enter "fishschools" into the search box.

❸ Choose your book to see a list of websites.

FACT
SURFER